A LIFE
WITH A
PURPOSE

How Cerebral Palsy Enabled Me
To Become *The Man I Am Today*

DEVAN STUGGIS

authorHOUSE

AuthorHouse™
1663 Liberty Drive
Bloomington, IN 47403
www.authorhouse.com
Phone: 833-262-8899

Published by AuthorHouse 08/28/2020

ISBN: 978-1-7283-7227-3 (sc)
ISBN: 978-1-7283-7226-6 (e)

Print information available on the last page.

This book is printed on acid-free paper.

DEDICATION

People with disabilities, A disability is just a physical condition; it doesn't define who we are as a person. We only have limitations. It doesn't stop us from living a productive life, so follow your dreams. We control our destiny, and life is full of opportunities. Never tell yourself that you can't do something because there is always a way to achieve it. If you fail, try again and again. Even though we have a disability, we can attain our goals and reach for the stars. Make sure that the stars are reachable. We have to be realistic.

PREFACE

One day I was in bed when I decided to write a book about my life. Minutes later, I called my best friend, Tom, and told him that I just decided to write a book about my life and ask him if he would be willing to help me write it. Tom said yes, I would help you, and it is a great idea. Tom, help me write most of the book. It took me eight years to complete it because self-doubt started to set in a few months after we began writing, and people started saying that I wouldn't finish the book. There were times when I wanted to stop working on it.the self-doubt and people talking were too much for me to handle, but I couldn't let what people said get to me. People not believing in me was my motivation to complete the book. Writing this book was a lot of fun.

My name is Devan Stuggis. I was born on January 9, 1986, in Fort Lauderdale, Florida. I have a younger sister, her name is Shaniqua .my mother had me when she was 21 years old. Five years later, she had my sister. We would have had an older brother; his name would have been Jarvis. He passed away because he was born prematurely; it would have been nice to have him around. We would be talking about everything that brothers talk about, but unfortunately, his life was cut short. I believe if Jarvis were here today, we would be so close I could just imagine what we would do if he were here we probably would be like Batman and Robin.

I was born with a disability called spastic cerebral palsy. The reason I was born with this disability is because my brain was bleeding from an aneurysm. My mother found out I had spastic cerebral palsy when I was nine months old due to my disability. I am physically dependent. Being physically dependent on others is very frustrating at times, but I don't let it get me down.

Spastic cerebral palsy affects all four limbs of my body due to my disability. I have limited use of my hands. I can write with my left hand., but it takes me a long time. When I write with a pen or pencil, it slows me down. I prefer typing on my laptop. Typing is a little bit faster for me, and I try to take my laptop wherever I go.because it has become a part of my day to day routine. My laptop is like my best friend. I don't know what I would do without it.

People underestimate me too much, and that irritates me. They also let my disability fool them; that's because they are just looking at my power chair. My chair helps me be more independent. It goes seven miles per hour. I wish it could go 70 miles per hour. Then I would feel like I am driving a real car. If I could drive, I would have a red BMW with leather seats with my name in the middle of the places and two TVs in the headrest. My car would be like my girlfriend. I would go for a lot of joyrides. My car would be my man cave, and I would spend a lot of time playing Xbox one in it.

On September 22, 2016, I received my new power wheelchair and I was so excited. I had to wait six years because there were some bumps in the road that delayed my chair. When I first got my chair, I fell asleep in it for a couple of hours. It felt good to be on my new ride. I couldn't wait for the next day to show it off. The new chair is a little bit faster than the old one. My old chair is more durable than the new one. I still have the old one just if the new one breaks down, thank God for that. From time to time, I can control the new chair better than the old one. That's because I can adjust the joystick to where I want it. I wish my new chair were able to raise so I could get stuff out of the kitchen and even cook something to eat with assistance. The first thing that I would cook is spaghetti. Garlic bread and spaghetti is one of my favorite foods to eat; it tastes good and even better with hot sauce. The type of power chair wheelchair that raises will help me be even more independent.

I don't like being in a power chair because I have to depend on people to help me. That's the hardest part about having a disability. I am so thankful for the help that I receive every day. I love that my power chair takes me wherever I want to go whenever I get tried, and I can tilt my chair back and relax for a few minutes. Sometimes I even take a nap in this position. That's How comfortable my chair is, Tilting my chair. Takes pressure off my butt, I sit in my power chair for hours. Taking pressure off my but prevents my skin from breaking down, I try to tilt my chair back every 2 hours. People think that my power chair is cool because it can lean back.

I need help getting in and out of bed, using the restroom. I also need help getting in and out of my power chair, Taking a shower and getting dressed. I wish I could do those things by myself. Sometimes I feel like I am getting on people's nerves when I ask for help. I cannot walk; I used to be able to take steps if someone holds me up.

Now I am not able to because my muscles are weak due to all of the operations I had over the years. Before the services, I was able to get out of my wheelchair onto the floor and move around. My mother couldn't keep me off the floor. I miss having the ability to do those things. The operations changed my life after my last surgery. I said to my doctor no more body had enough.

My mother was a single parent for the majority of our lives. My father wasn't there for me my whole childhood; I used to tell people I didn't have a father, I have a sperm donor, and I was affected by him not being there for me. I used to think that he didn't want anything to do with me because of my disability. There were nights when I would cry. The reason my father wasn't there for me he was in prison for possession of cocaine. I feel like he put cocaine before me. I forgive my father for not being there for me because we all make bad choices in life.No one is perfect. He is no longer in prison, We don't have a relationship, and that's all I ever wanted. If God blesses me with kids, I won't do them the same way that my father did me. Thank God for Shaniqua" s father; he was there for me until I was eight years old. He showed me what a loving father looks like, so in my heart, he" s my father I was so hurt when our father moved back home to Connecticut. We had a lot of fun as a family after our parents broke up; my mother struggled to take care of us.

Shaniqua was like my other mother. She helped our mother take care of me growing up. We were very close. Everything changed when my mother decided to send her to live with our father because she wasn't doing well. I could tell that she didn't want to go.i had a feeling that the move to Connecticut would affect our relationship. We did everything together. We learned to visit our great-grandmother almost every weekend that was my favorite thing to do,

My great-grandmother was a very loving, caring person to be around. She was my best friend. My great-grandmother passed away during stomach surgery at the age of 88 I enjoyed every minute I spent with her. My great-grandmother always made me laugh; she was an excellent cook. Whatever she cooked tasted very good, my great-grandmother cooked everything from scratch. I loved when she made cornbread and collard greens I always wanted seconds. Cooking with her favorite thing to do, My great-grandmother had to raise my mother, sisters, and brothers because my grandmother passed away. My mother was nine years old when my grandmother passed away, and she had nine kids, seven girls, and two boys. My mother is the second youngest girl in the family. My great-grandmother did an excellent job raising them.

My mother also grew up without her father. Thanks to my great-grandmother, My mother and sisters turned out to be successful women. If I could walk, I would be a hard worker, just like my mother. She always told my sister and me to strive to be successful, and that's what I try to do every day of my life. My mother sacrificed a lot for us, so we could have whatever we needed or wanted to get what we wished we had to do well in school by bringing home a sound report card. My mother didn't play when it came to school. On school nights, we had to be in bed at nine. The only time We didn't go to bed at nine is if we still have homework. Homework was the first thing we had to do when we got home from school.

My whole family used to go on trips every year. My favorite place to travel to was Georgia. We used to go there in the wintertime. We have family there whenever we went there. I liked going to toA restaurant called Waffle House for breakfast. My favorite breakfast to order cheese grits with eggs and sausage. It tastes so good. We used to take boxes of sausages and biscuits home with us to Florida. I loved riding my power chair on the dirt roads and talking sports with my family. Georgia was like my home away from home.

I went to a particular school for people with disabilities. It was so lovely to be around other people with the same disability as me. I went there until I was ten years old because my mother felt like I wasn't learning anything, so she decided to put me in public school. I adjusted to my new school well, from the first day I started I learned so much more than I did at my other school. The curriculum was very different. The curriculum was so much better for me because it made me use my brain more. Every day I saw improvement in education. I looked forward to going to school every day because I was learning a whole lot more. If I missed a day of school, I used to get so mad. I used to have a unique aide that helped me with everything.

Everything changed when I got to middle school. I started hanging out with the wrong people, skipping class, and using profanity, I was a handful. The school couldn't find anyone to work with me because of my behavior. When I got to school one morning, my teacher came up to me and said I want to introduce you to your new unique aide; his name is Tom. He will be working with you from now on. Tom shook my hand, and then we talked for a few minutes before I started my work. It took me about a month to get used to him, from the first day he started working with me. I could tell that it was his first time working as a unique aide.

Tom was a different story; he worked with me for three years. Tom was a fascinating person, but we got along pretty well. When he became my aide, I started to change my behavior. However, there were still times when I would go back to doing the same things. My friends used to say to me, "Boy, if you weren't in a wheelchair, you would have a lot of girlfriends" People still tell me that today. If I were able to walk, I would be talking to girls, but I don't have many girlfriends. The only thing that would be on my mind was making money. Back when I was in middle school, girls were the only thing that I was worried about, school wasn't necessary to me anymore. During this time, I wasn't in the right frame of mind because of my friends. I don't know how Tom put up with me for three years because I gave him a hard time some days, he didn't mind. Thank God that he didn't quit on me like the people before him. Tom had a lot of patience. He used to do an exercise called TAI Chi while waiting for me to arrive. I laugh until my stomach hurts and looks at him crazy because I never heard or saw anyone do Tai Chi before. Seeing Tom do Tai chi every morning was my entertainment.

After my freshman year, my mother moved us to Riviera Beach. Moving there got me back on track in school. My teachers were more strict, so I had no choice but to get myself together. During this time, I realized that my behavior wasn't going to help me reach my goal. My goal was to drive across the stage and get my diploma, two years after moving back to Fort Lauderdale, I accomplished my goal. I graduated from Fort

Lauderdale high school with a 3.0-grade point average, if it wasn't for Tom, my teachers and mother moving us away, I probably wouldn't have reached my goal. I thank God for my teachers, holding me accountable for my actions, that what I needed. When I graduated, I don't know who was the happiest; me or my aunt Brenda! She was the loudest one in the auditorium. It felt so good to drive my wheelchair across the stage.

On March 4, 2006, I moved from my mother's house into a group home because I wanted to be more independent, and my sister no longer lived with us. I lived in the group home with five other people that have Cerebral palsy just like me. It took me a few months to get used to the group home, and I lived there for five years. One of the people that I lived with is my best friend, Danielle. She was so happy to see me; we went to elementary school together. I was the only one in the group home that could talk, being the only one there that could speak wasn't a problem for me at all.

The group home staff was nice, and they treated me well. The group homeowner and group home staff took Danielle and me to a Miami Heat game. tWe had a good time. Danielle and I also went to a Beyonce concert, which was also the first time going to a show. I am one of her biggest fans; we enjoyed every minute of the concert. Seeing Beyonce in person was a dream come true. I wish we had backstage passes that night that would have been awesome to sit down and talk to her and take a picture together.

Danielle and I used to do everything together. Our favorite things to do together or watch movies and go to the mall we also liked going to church with my best friend Christian. He also has cerebral palsy Christian reminds me a lot of myself in so many ways one way he reminds me of myself is that he's very determined; that's one of the things that I like about him. Christian Is a very caring person and a chameleon. It was a joy to be around him Christian Now lives in New York with his family. We talk on the phone all the time. When he lived in Florida, we hung out all the time. Christian was always on the go. He's a very adventurous person with a lot of confidence. Christian doesn't let cerebral palsy slow him down; 'I am glad to have Christian us as my friend.

I thank God every day for the ability to move around with the help of my power chair. People ask me all the time if I feel sorry for myself because I have a disability. I have them know God wanted me to be this way. When I am in public people stop and stare at me like they never saw a person in a power chair before that irritates me, People, Sometimes ask was in a car accident I say no I was born with a disability called cerebral palsy.

At the age of 21, I started going to a day program for people with disabilities. That's where I met my best friend, Christian. We were in the same class. I went there five days a week for three years. A lot of my friends that I know from elementary school go there. I left the program because it was time for a change. When I was there, my best friend Ryan started going to the program we met in elementary school.

Ryan introduced me to his best friend, Brian, when they came over to the group home to watch a football game with me. Ryan and I used to race our power chairs In the school hallways at full speed. I was known as a speed racer because I always drive my power chair fast. Months after Ryan introduced me to his friend Brian we began friends; he came to see me all the time. We used to play games on my Xbox One. Our favorite game to play was the Madden team that he liked to use was New England. I used the Denver Broncos or the Kansas City Chiefs. Those are my two favorite teams Brian, and I always had debates. Because he thinks that the New England Patriots are the best team in the world, they are good, but they are not the best team in the world a lot of their success It's because of Tom Brady I want to see how good New England would be if he decided to retire or go to a different team If that happens New England will not win another Super Bowl for a long time every time we played madden Brian brat me he's a good video game player I have to be in the mood to play in my Xbox One I used to wait until Brian came over to the group home to play my Xbox One because it was so much playing against him.

I went to another day program for people with disabilities five days a week. Every morning we did academic stuff. Every client had to do personal goals for 12 days a month. We went on trips twice a week When we weren't able to go on trips, we did word searches or had a class discussion on different topics after lunch we played games or watched movies a week once a month we had a cooking class. My teacher cooked simple meals. She is an excellent cook. I learned when she made salmon cakes and empanadas also smoothies. I looked forward to having a cooking class every month. The staff in the classroom was very caring and helpful. The only thing that I didn't like about the program is we didn't get a lot of days off.

On March 15, 2008, I meant a woman on the chat line I was home bored, so I went on there To find someone to talk to The woman started sending me messages We sent messages back and forth for a while then we decided to exchange members she seemed like a down-to-earth person We talked for hours that night. When we met for the first time, I was so nervous. It was love at first sight. I don't date women because they look good or have a beautiful body. Looks don't tell me anything about a woman; the woman that I met on the chat line was my first relationship. It started on the wrong foot because I didn't tell her that I have a disability right away. I was afraid that she wouldn't talk to me anymore. It took me five months after we started dating to tell her that I have a disability; she was mad, not telling her that I was so immature of me initially. I was surprised we stayed together after I told her. I tried to date other women before her, but they didn't want to date me because of my disability. My girlfriend looked past my disability. I never thought I would find a girlfriend because of my disability. Unfortunately, we moved too fast Into a relationship looking back. It wasn't a real relationship because we didn't spend a lot of time together. After all, she lived in another part of Florida when we did spend time together, and we had a great time.

Three years into our relationship, I ran away from the group home for three days to spend time with her. We stayed at the Hilton Hotel. I paid $300. Only a couple of my friends knew where I was. Everyone was looking for me. That was the longest time we ever spent together. I wanted to make a memorable moment. I lost my Virginia on the first night. I surprised myself by making a big decision like that since that night I haven't been sexually active with another woman Losing my virginity with something that I wanted to do with a woman that loves me, but it didn't happen that way. We got lost on the way to my mother's house, that was the most embarrassing date of my life.

We walked all day trying to get to my mother's house. I called my sister and told her that we were lost; she asked me who I am with and where we are trying to go. I am with my girlfriend. We are trying to go to my mother's house. My sister called our aunt to pick us up. I didn't want my mother to find out, but she had already found out all hell broke loose when my mother got to the group home. She gave t/he group owner a piece of her mind. My girlfriend was so mad at me that, 30 minutes after speaking with my sister, my aunt and cousins were there to pick us up. They were so surprised to see my girlfriend. They asked a lot of questions. I felt like I was in a courtroom. I wasn't ready for the questions to end. When we got to the group home, there were many police there. I never saw so many police in my life. My mother wanted to fight my girlfriend because she didn't know if I was hurt. I put everyone in a bad position when I ran the way that was very inconsiderate of me. I am lucky that she let me continue to live at the group home after that crazy night.

A month after that crazy night, I lost contact with my girlfriend. I searched all over the internet for her every day that went by made me scared that she might be in another relationship. I reached a dark place in my life a month after we got back together. One day when I came home from the casino, I tried to kill myself with a fork. Later that night, I tried to do it with my phone charger. The baker acted when I came home from the day program. The group homeowner came to my room and asked me if I still feel like killing myself. I said yes, then I was baker acted, and I felt like I was in jail. I was there for 7 hours, but it felt longer than that I was so ready to go home. The hospital doctor sent me to a psychiatrist. The next day I went to see the psychiatrist. He told me I was suffering from depression and suggested that I go into group treatment. I went to the group twice a week for two months. I was nervous about going to group treatment. Going to the group helped me. The hardest part was accepting that I had a problem. The only thing I didn't like about croup treatments was I had to take medication. The only thing the medication did for me made me gain weight and sleep all-day. It also made me isolate myself from everyone. I only came out of my room when it was time for dinner or when I had to go to my day program. There were days when I didn't even want to go because I didn't have the energy to do anything. I stopped taking the medication for those reasons. My family was so against me taking the medication, especially my aunt Brenda. She was outraged at me when she found out that I tried to kill myself. She told me to stop taking the medication because I was looking like a zombie.

If it weren't for me wanting to change my life and the group treatment, I would still be gambling and depressed. Thank God that I got my life together before it was too late. I am ashamed of myself because of what I tried to do to myself. What I have done has made me a wiser person. I am proud of myself for overcoming my gambling addiction. There were times when I wanted to quit the group because I didn't have any money for transportation. I knew that I couldn't let money stop me from going to the treatment group because it might be the only way to beat my addiction.

A year after I finished their treatment group, I became a volunteer for Memorial Regional Hospital at the outpatient behavioral health facility twice a week after the day program. Volunteering gave me something to do. I did it for four years. The reason I stopped is that

I wasn't interested in doing it anymore. A few months later, my mother found out that she has breast cancer. When she told me The lousy news, I was confused. I started crying, hearing that news made me depressed. All I could think about at that time was what's going to happen to me if she doesn't beat breast cancer. Thank God, my mother beat breast cancer. Breast cancer runs in my family. Seeing my mother going through cancer was very difficult for me. Now I have a new outlook on life.

My family used to tell me I don't have a life. Every time they used to say to me, I used to laugh, but they were right. I thought my family was just telling me I don't have a life to try to stop going on the chat line. The chat line was my entertainment. I know it sounds crazy. It is the craziest thing that I have ever tried in my life. I don't know why I was in such a hurry to start dating. It wasn't a good idea because I wasn't ready and too immature. Thank God that my mother didn't give up on me at times I thought she would because I gave her a hard time when they came to who I was dating. My mother couldn't tell me anything, Whatever she told me went in one ear and out the other because I thought she was trying to control my dating life. I didn't realize how much the chat line and my girlfriend at the time were influencing my mind. That's when I decided to focus on myself and stop worrying about women who don't care about me. It was difficult for me to get to that point.ita not the end of the world if I don't have a girlfriend. If a woman loves and cares about me, she shouldn't be taking advantage of me. It took me a while to get that through my head. A woman doesn't do what I allow her to do. It was an uphill battle for me to get myself mentally strong. My ex-girlfriend knew that I had a soft spot for her; she took advantage of that. I felt less of a man every day. My mother cried; she told me that she prays to God that I would change. I hit rock bottom before I saw everything that my mother and my aunt Brenda told me along. They were so happy when I turned my life around. If I had listened to them, I wouldn't have to pee and all of that drama. I feel bad that they had to see me go through all that drama for all those years. If it weren't for God and my mother, I wouldn't be able to turn my life around.

On March 18, 2011, I moved out of the group home into my place. I loved living on my own. Living on my own was always a dream of mine. I felt like a real man and more independent. My aunt Brenda helped me get my place. She laid around the corner from me. I had mixed emotions when I moved out of the group home. It was hard for me to tell my friend Danielle. I won't be living there anymore. She begged me to stay. I told her that I couldn't pass up this opportunity. She wished me well, and she said to me that it wouldn't be the same without me, It hurt me so much to see Danielle crying when I left, She was so upset she didn't even tell me goodbye. Every time I went to visit, everyone was happy to see me. Danielle always used to ask me when am I going to move back. I always used to tell her that I miss her, but I loveLiving on my own While living in the group home, I learned how to speak Creole. I don't speak it fluently, or is that much? When I speak Creole, people think that I am from Haiti; they don't believe me when I say that I am not from Haiti. I love speaking Creole.

On August 6, 2013, my aunt Brenda passed away from a massive heart attack. She was 54 years old. Two days before she passed away, she came over to my home to see my mother and me after she left work. We had a long conversation that day. After all these years, I still can't believe that my aunt is no longer here. Every year When the anniversary of her passing comes, I am sad and depressed. I know she's in heaven looking down. I miss her so much, and I wish she were still here. My aunt Brenda was my best friend. We talked about everything.

My favorite thing to discuss with her was politics. I find politics interesting, but I don't always agree with what the politicians say most of the time. Some of them are only looking out for themselves; they are not looking out for people like me With disabilities. Some politicians want to make things harder for people with disabilities to get the services that we need. I also like to talk to my friends about politics just to get their opinions on specific issues, Most of the time we agree on the same things, Whenever my aunt

Brenda didn't call me I knew that something was wrong so I would call her to make sure that she was okay. She would do the same if I didn't call her or come over to my home. We spent a lot of time together. My aunt came to my home almost every day. I enjoyed every minute that we spent together even though we had arguments about my girlfriend. My aunt didn't like her because she thought that my girlfriend was taking advantage of me. Every time my aunt told me that it made me so angry. She was right all along, but I was too blind to see what my girlfriend was doing to me. My relationship is a subject that I don't like to talk about with anyone. My aunt Brenda looked out for me. I loved it when she came over to watch Tennis in the Miami Heat games with me.

My aunt Brenda would be so happy I know that My girlfriend broke up with me because things didn't go the way that she planned when she came down to see me, so she wanted to go home after I almost paid $200 for her to come down to see me. We only spent 24 hours together. I was so disappointed. I could have used that money to pay a bill. By her wanting to go home, she showed me that our relationship was a joke to her. I loved her, and I hoped that she would change. Our relationship was all about what I can do for her. I only heard from her when she needed money. She wasn't the right woman for me. It took me seven years to realize that.bi was disappointed with myself for a long time.

I met a new woman a year later after my ex-girlfriend broke up with me. She was nothing like my ex-girlfriend; I was so much happier with her. I met her at a Halloween party. We had a long pleasant conversation at the Halloween party. All I could think about that night when I got home was the conversation that we had. We started dating on November 2, 2014; We saw each other almost every. My love for her grew every day. She showed me a lot of love and treated me like a king. My girlfriend loved me. She is a very independent woman. I finally got a taste of real love from a real woman, which I thought was never possible. It was nice to know that I could count on my girlfriend all time and not have to worry about anything as long as she was around. Unfortunately, nine months into the relationship, we broke up because she told me she didn't have time for a relationship. I also thought that she was the one for me. Thank God she was honest with me and not lead me on.

I wish that my first ex-girlfriend would have done the same thing. She actually broke my heart. That's not the way love works. She made me grow up fast. Now I know the signs of an unhealthy relationship. My ex-girlfriend causes me to have low self-esteem and almost give up on love. After we broke up, I told myself a real woman is in my future. When she comes into my life, I hope she treats me well. Due to the way my first ex-girlfriend treated me, I have my walls up. Some of the pain was my fault because I jumped into the relationship without really getting to know the first two women I allowed to come into my life. That was my biggest problem. As soon as they told me that they love me, they have my heart. That's how bad I wanted to be in a relationship. Growing up, I always told myself and my mother that I wouldn't let women take advantage of meI don't know what made them gullible. My mother didn't raise me to be that way; I am smarter than that. People used to tell me that I am not the same person. Whenever people set it, I felt terrible, but Not enough to break up with my first ex-girlfriend. All I was worried about was my relationship with her. I almost lost everything because I've put her before me. By doing this, I made her feel like she was on top of the world; she didn't deserve to feel that way. My first girlfriend is a great Pretender. If there were an award for a great pretender, she would win, and she would be a great candidate.

On December 22, 2015, I started dating my best friend, Ellen, from high school. I have a big crush on her back then. I didn't know how to tell her How I felt; We were in the same class, and we sat right across from one another. It was hard for me to do my classwork. Whenever I needed something, she was the one I asked to get whatever I needed. I couldn't wait to go to school the next day. I had a crush on Ellen all those years, even though I was dating other women. The thing that I like about Ellen the most is she's accommodating and caring. It's not easy to find women with those qualities. I understand that every woman is different; I have to protect my heart. I took my time with this relationship and asked God to guide me because when I move fast, the relationship doesn't end well.

One day I saw her brother at the place where I used to volunteer, that was my first time meeting him. The next time he came, he told me his sister remembered me from high school. I was so happy and surprised to hear that she reminded me. When her brother told me those words, it brought tears to my eyes. After that day, all I wanted was to see her again. I got what I wanted two weeks later when I went to volunteer there. I was so happy to see her for the first time after all those years. She didn't say too much to me. I was surprised to see that she still looks the same. Unfortunately, four years into the relationship, My life was turned upside down because we broke up. People told me that Ellen had a new boyfriend when I heard that my heart broke. My moon intuition tells me that that's not true. People said to me that lame story too got me out of her life, made a good couple. If it weren't for people in the future in our relationship, we would still be together today; We were doing just fine until that lame story came out in my heart, she is still my girlfriend. The feelings I have for Ellen will never change, and no other woman will get the opportunity to get close to my heart because Ellen will always be there. I miss her company, and every second of every day, it plans me every day the way our relationship.

On September 20, 2017. I decided to move back to the group home because I didn't feel safe staying at my place during hurricane Irma, another reason I decided to move back is that after my lease would have been up, I wouldn't have the money to move to another place. My aunt Brenda not being here anymore played a part in my decision. One day she said to me, everything is going to change if something ever happens to me. I miss living on my own so much because I don't have the responsibilities that I have before. Now, I feel less of a man because of the decision I made. The decision hurts me every day. I can't believe that I gave up my place. When moving back to the group home was the right thing to do. I feel like I let my family down when I made my decision, especially my aunt Brenda. I know she's in heaven so mad that I gave up on my dream that she helped me accomplish. My aunt Brenda wouldn't be able to forgive me or talk to me if she were still alive today.

Two years later, I moved back to the group home. I welcomed two new additions to my life. I got two baby parakeets, a boy and a girl named our precious and Max. It's a real joy to have them a part of my life. The day before I got my birds I couldn't sleep because I was so excited, it felt like my birthday was the next day. Every time precious and Max sees me. They make noise. Other than that, they are quite dead birds. Every morning and afternoon, I spend about 30 minutes outside with him to make sure they have food and water. Sometimes I take them out of their cage and put them on my lap. My boobs are my babies; having them in my life gives me responsibility. I love my responsibility so much, and I would never give up my beds for anything in the world—the reason I got a princess and Maxis for the company because I felt very lonely.

ACKNOWLEDGMENT

I want to start by saying my book wouldn't be in your hands today if it weren't for God, giving me the strength to finish it. Words can't express how thankful I am for the Publishing Company to share my story with the world. My aunt Brenda gave me the confidence to start on his journey; If she were here, she would be so happy to know that I finished something that I started. I am the man I am today because of my mother and the things that I have been through in my life. It feels good to be an author. I hope you all enjoyed my book.